Gravity

Contents

D0095941

written by Dawn McMillan

1

Gravity is an invisible force of nature. A force is a push or a pull. Gravity is a pull. If you throw a stone in the air, it will fall down because it is pulled by the Earth's gravity.

When you fall off your bike or spill your drink, gravity is at work! Gravity is what makes things fall down to Earth.

forces

It was a famous scientist, called <u>Isaac Newton</u>, who first thought about gravity. One day, when he was sitting under an apple tree, an apple fell on his head.

He wondered why the apple fell down. Why didn't it go up, or sideways? This made him think that something pulled the apple down.

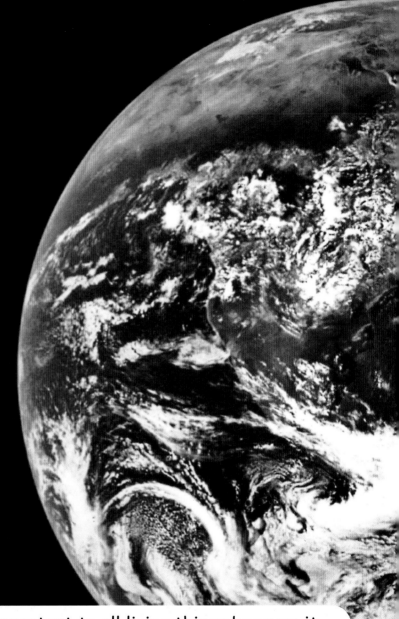

Gravity is important to all living things because it keeps us in place on Earth. If gravity didn't pull us down, we would float off the planet.

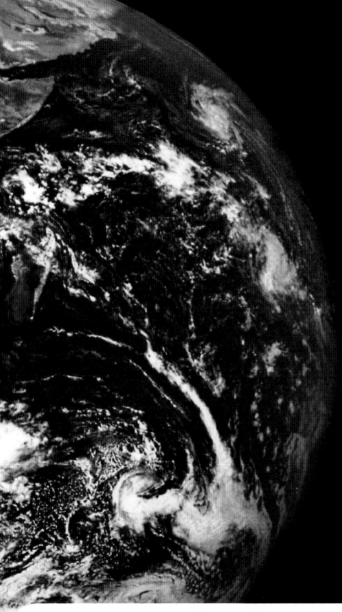

All our water would float off, too, and even the air that we need to breathe would float away!

Gravity pulls things closer to each other. If an apple falls off a tree, both Earth and the apple are pulling each other. But we don't notice the tiny pull of the apple because Earth is huge, and it has a very strong pull.

When gravity pulls on your body, it is called weight. The further away from the centre of Earth you are, the less you weigh. If you were on a mountain top, you would weigh a little less.

Things like wood, stone, and water are made from very tiny particles. Even air is made up from little particles. We are also made from particles, but they are too small for us to see.

The more particles something has, the more gravity pulls on it. That is what makes things feel heavy.

particles

The pull of the Moon's gravity is less than Earth's gravity because the Moon is smaller. Whatever you weigh on Earth, you would weigh six times less on the Moon.

That means that you could jump six times as high there as you could on Earth. If you went to Pluto, you would weigh twelve times less. How high could you jump there?

Our Earth pulls on the Moon, and the Moon pulls on Earth. It is Earth's gravity that keeps the Moon moving around us. As the Moon goes around Earth, it pulls the sea closer to it. This makes the tide high. Once the Moon is past the sea, the water falls back again and the tide is low.

The Sun is more than 100 times bigger than Earth, and its gravity is very strong. It holds Earth and all the other planets in their orbits or they would float off into space.

Gravity is amazing! But if you want to live without it, learn to be an astronaut. There is no gravity out in space, so there is no 'down'. How do you think that would feel?